SOUND
—AND—
HEARING

VOLUME 8

Chris Woodford

GROLIER
EDUCATIONAL

Published 2002 by Grolier Educational
Sherman Turnpike,
Danbury, Connecticut 06816

FOR BROWN PARTWORKS

Project editor:	Lisa Magloff
Deputy editor:	Jane Scarsbrook
Text editors:	Caroline Beattie, Chris Cooper
Designer:	Joan Curtis
Picture researcher:	Liz Clachan
Illustrations:	Mark Walker
Index:	Kay Ollerenshaw
Design manager:	Lynne Ross
Production manager:	Matt Weyland
Managing editor:	Bridget Giles
Editorial director:	Anne O'Daly
Consultant:	Martyn D. Wheeler, PhD University of Leicester

Printed and bound in Hong Kong

Set ISBN 0-7172-5608-1
Volume ISBN 0-7172-5616-2

Library of Congress Cataloging-in-Publication Data
Science Activities / Grolier Educational
    p. cm.
    Includes index.
    Contents: v.1. Electricity and magnetism—v.2. Everyday Chemistry—v.3. Force and
motion—v.4. Heat and energy—v.5. Inside matter—v.6. Light and color—v.7. Our
Environment—v.8. Sound and hearing—v.9. Using materials—v.10. Weather and climate.
ISBN 0-7172-5608-1 (set : alk.paper)—ISBN 0-7172-5609-X (v.1 : alk. paper)—
ISBN 0-7172-5610-3 (v.2 : alk. paper)—ISBN 0-7172-5611-1 (v.3 : alk. paper)—ISBN
0-7172-5612-X (v.4 : alk. paper)—ISBN 0-7172-5613-8 (v.5 : alk. paper)—ISBN
0-7172-5614- 6 (v.6 : alk. paper)—ISBN 0-7172-5615-4 (v.7 : alk. paper)—ISBN
0-7172-5616-2 (v.8 : alk. paper)—ISBN 0-7172-5617-0 (v.9 : alk. paper)—ISBN
0-7172-5618-9 (v.10 : alk. paper)
    1. Science—Study and teaching—Activity programs—Juvenile literature. [1.
Science—Experiments. 2. Experiments] I. Grolier Educational (Firm)

LB1585.S335 2002
507.1'2—dc21

2001040519

ABOUT THIS SET

Science Activities gives children a chance to explore fascinating topics from the world of science using the same methods that professional scientists use to solve problems. This set introduces young scientists to the scientific method by focusing on the importance of planning experiments, conducting them in a rigorous fashion so that a fair test can be carried out, recording all the stages, and organizing and analyzing the data to draw conclusions. Readers will have the chance to conduct exciting and innovative hands-on activities and to learn how to record and analyze their experiments and results in a variety of ways.

Every volume of *Science Activities* contains 10 step-by-step experiments, along with follow-up activities that encourage readers to find out more about the subject. The activities are explained and enhanced with detailed introductory and analysis sections. Colorful photos illustrate each activity, and every book is packed full of pictures and illustrations explaining the details of each topic.

By working fun and educational experiments into the context of the scientific method, anyone using this set can get a feel for how professional scientists go about their work. Most importantly, just have fun!

PICTURE CREDITS
(b=bottom; t=top; l=left; r=right)

Art Explosion: 23; **Corbis:** Craig Aurness front cover, CRDPHOTO 5, Kevin Fleming 35, Mitchell Gerber 12, Richard T. Nowitz 11, 56, Neal Preston 24, Kim Sayer 55, Ted Streshinsky 34, Nubar Alexanian 39(b), Eric & David Hosking 17(b), Adam Woolfit 51(b), David Reed 39(t), W.P Zuber 17(t); **Ecoscene:** Alan Towse 51 (t); **Empics:** Jed Leicester 7; **GKN Westland Helicopters:** 49; **Hulton Archive:** 18, 29, 41; **Image Bank:** Jeff Hunter 19, Paul McCormick 4; **NASA:** 23(r); Sony: 13 (r), 13(l); **Science Photo Library:** 61(r), Tek Image 6, US Geological Survey 13 (b), Space Telescope Science Institute/NASA 61(r); **Surrey Police:** Stan Gillingham 57; **Sylvia Cordaiy:** Chris Parker 50, Johnathan Smith 45; **Travel Ink:** Charlie Marsden 40.

CONTENTS

VOLUME 8
SOUND AND HEARING

INTRODUCTION

Sounds are vibrations in the air. Every time something moves, it makes a sound, from a butterfly flapping its wings to an airplane taking off. The world is full of different sounds that reach our ears.

We are surrounded by sounds. Sound makes it possible for us to communicate with other people, even when we can't see them, to make music others can hear, to laugh and share jokes, and even to sense danger and react quickly. Many other animals use sound, too. Birds sing to attract mates. Bats find their way around using very high-pitched squeaks called ultrasound (above the pitch that people can hear). Whales communicate with one another across hundreds of miles of ocean using low-pitched moans called infrasound (below the pitch that people can hear).

THE SCIENCE OF SOUND

Sound is made when objects vibrate (move back and forth quickly). If you rest one of your fingers gently on your throat while you are speaking or singing a song, you can feel your vocal cords vibrating; these vibrations produce your voice. The same thing happens when you pluck the string of a guitar. The string moves rapidly from side to side, creating the musical note.

Coyotes howl to communicate with one another. Like most animals, the coyote has a range of sounds that it can make, and each one has a different meaning.

You can hear someone singing or plucking a guitar string because the sound travels out from where it is made and into your ears. Sound is a type of energy that travels between two places by making invisible waves in the air, a bit like the waves that travel across the sea. Imagine someone playing a guitar across the room from you. Now imagine waves of sound, like the waves on the sea, traveling through the air from the guitar to your ears.

The sound waves you can hear when someone plucks a guitar string are collected by your ears and turned into information that your brain can understand. Having two ears means your brain can figure out where sounds are coming from and pinpoint the source of a sound very accurately. Some animals, such as rabbits, can lift up their ears and move them around to locate sounds even more accurately. Other animals, like dogs, are sensitive to sounds that people can't hear.

FINDING OUT ABOUT SOUND

The ten activities in this book will help you find out for yourself what sound is all about. You will learn what sound waves are and why they behave as they do, how they travel in different ways, and how to make sound waves of different kinds.

Each activity involves doing an experiment—a test carried out by a scientist to find out why the world behaves in the way that it does. Many of the things people know about the world have been found out using what is called the scientific method. It involves scientists trying to understand something by making observations (perhaps by looking at or listening to something or carefully making measurements). When scientists think they have an idea why things work as they do, that is called a theory. Once they have a theory, scientists think up experiments to test whether the theory is correct. They gradually change the theory until it explains the results of all their experiments.

🔊 *Concert halls, like the Sydney Opera House (above), are designed to be both attractive and to reflect sound waves in such a way as to produce excellent sound.*

The good science guide

Science is not only a collection of facts—it is the process that scientists use to gather information. Follow this good science guide to get the most out of each experiment.

● Carry out each experiment more than once. That prevents accidental mistakes skewing the results. The more times you carry out an experiment, the easier it will be to see if your results are accurate.
● Decide how you will write down your results. You can use a variety of different methods, such as descriptions, diagrams, tables, charts, and graphs. Choose the methods that will make your results easy to read and understand.
● Be sure to write your results down as you are doing the experiment. If one of the results seems very different from the others, it could be because of a problem with the experiment that you should fix immediately.
● Drawing a graph of your results can be very useful because it helps fill in the gaps in your experiment. Imagine, for example, that you plot time along the bottom of the graph and temperature up the side. If you measure the temperature ten times, you can put the results on the graph as dots. Use a ruler to draw a straight line through all the dots. You can now estimate what happened in between each dot, or measurement, by picking any point along the line and reading the time and temperature for that point from the sides of the graph.
● Learn from your mistakes. Some of the most exciting findings in science came from an unexpected result. If your results do not tally with your predictions, try to find out why.
● You should always be careful when carrying out or preparing any experiment, whether it is dangerous or not. Make sure you know the safety rules before you start working.
● Never begin an experiment until you have talked to an adult about what you are going to do.

ACTIVITY 1
SOUND WAVES

Most sounds reach our ears as they travel in waves through the air. However, sounds also travel through liquids and solids. Even when you are under water in the swimming pool or bath—you can still hear sounds.

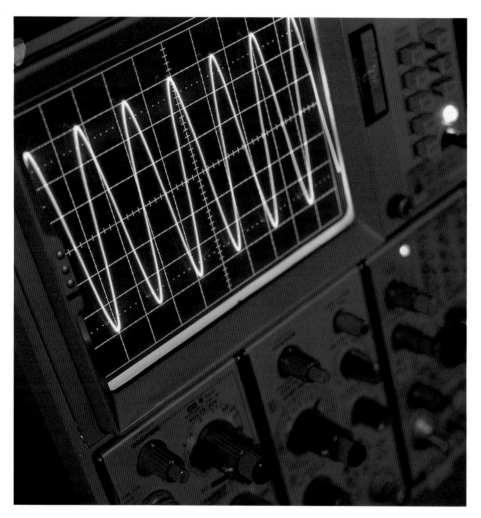

An ocilloscope is a device for "seeing" sound waves. The oscilloscope draws a picture of what the sound wave would look like if we could see it. The taller the waves, the louder the sound.

If you sit and listen to your TV, you might think the sound is traveling from the TV to your ears through empty space. In reality sounds from your TV are carried through the air in the room. Air is invisible; but if we could dye it so it showed up, you would be able to see sound waves traveling through the air a little like waves on the sea. The air particles would be bouncing back and forth, carrying sound energy from the TV to your ears. If you sucked all the air out of your living room, your TV would mysteriously go quiet. With no air in the room there would be nothing to carry the noise from the TV to your ears. Sound cannot travel through a vacuum (empty space). Sound must travel through a medium.

Ocean waves can travel over the water because the water makes a path over which waves can move, just as a highway is a path for cars. Without that path there would be nothing to make, or carry, the waves, and they could not travel. Sound waves also need a path to travel on. The path sound waves use is any substance the sound waves can move through. This substance is usually called a medium, and it can be many things, from air to iron.

TWO TYPES OF WAVES

Although sound waves are a lot like water waves, they are different in one very important way. Energy is carried through the ocean when areas of water move up and down in turn. Just like a crowd wave moving around a baseball stadium, areas of water seem to "stand up" and then "sit down" again. And just as the people don't move to the right or left during a stadium wave, the water doesn't move from one place to another in the ocean—it simply bobs up and down. This type of wave is called a transverse wave. The individual particles that make up such waves move at right angles to the direction in which the wave is traveling. Thus the people taking part in a stadium wave stand up and sit down while the wave moves along from left to right, or vice versa.

Sound waves are different. If you could see sound waves, they would look like a train locomotive backing into a line of cars. As the locomotive hits the first car, it pushes on that car's bumpers, compressing (squeezing) them a little. The first car then starts to move, pushing into the bumpers of the second car. The second car starts to move toward the third car, but the first car also bounces back a little toward the locomotive. If you look closely, you can see how the energy moves down

A stadium wave is a transverse wave—just like an ocean wave. As the people move up and down, a wave travels around the stadium.

the line, with some cars moving toward the locomotive, and some moving away, all at the same time. Some of the couplings between the cars appear to be expanding, while others appear to be compressing. When energy travels like this, it is called a longitudinal wave or a compression wave.

A sound wave is another example of a compression wave. But instead of being carried by locomotives and cars, sound waves are transmitted when air particles bounce back and forth. When sound moves in a compression wave, the individual air particles move back and forth in the same direction as the wave itself.

SEEING SOUNDS

It is not possible to see sound moving through air, but we can study sounds in other ways. Sound is made when objects vibrate, but sounds also make objects vibrate. That is one way to "see" sound. When opera singers sing, for example, they can sometimes make a wine glass vibrate and "sing," too. Another way of seeing sounds is to use a scientific instrument called an oscilloscope. It is an electronic device that automatically draws a graph of what a sound wave looks like on a small screen. In the following experiment you are going to build your own device for "seeing" sound waves.

Sound movement

As a sound wave moves through the air, it pushes air molecules in front of it. These particles of air then bump into more particles and push them along too, in a continuous wave. When this wave reaches your ear, you hear it as a sound.

Over time the wave will lose energy, becoming smaller, and finally flattening out. That's why, if a sound is too far away, you cannot hear it. The wave has lost energy, flattened out, and disappeared before it reaches your ear.

Bouncing Waves

Goals

1. Make a sound detector.
2. Use your detector to investigate different sound waves.

What you will need:

- white cardboard
- pen and pencil
- ruler
- balloon
- large can, open at both ends
- rubber band
- small mirror
- flashlight
- tape

Robert Boyle

Irish chemist Robert Boyle (1627–1691) was the first person to discover that sound needs a medium through which to travel. He set an alarm clock ringing in a large jar, then slowly pumped all the air out of it. When all the air had been sucked away, Boyle found he could no longer hear the clock.

1 Using the ruler, draw a grid of squares on the white cardboard. The sides of each square should be 2 inches (5cm) long. Fill the entire sheet of cardboard with your grid.

2 Cut the end off the balloon to make a single large sheet of rubber.

3 Carefully tape around any sharp edges on the can. Stretch the balloon over one end of the can. Use a rubber band to hold it down.

4 Tape the mirror to the balloon.

5 Prop your graph cardboard against a pile of books so that it is standing upright on a table. Place the can and flashlight on the table so that the light from the flashlight shines on the mirror and reflects onto the cardboard.

Troubleshooting

What if I can't see the light moving?

Try moving your flashlight so that it shines more directly on the mirror, and darken the room by turning out the lights. You might also try using a dark cardboard, and making lines with white tape. Or simply try making a louder sound.

6 Make a mark in the square the light is shining on.

7 While looking at the cardboard, hold your hands about 2 feet (60cm) from the can, and clap once. How far does the light move? Make a mark in the square the light moves into.

8 Now clap your hands together 6 inches (7.5cm) from the can. Make a mark in the square the light moves into.

9 Measure the distance between the original mark and each of the marks made when you clapped your hands. Compare how far the light jumped in each case.

FOLLOW-UP Bouncing waves

After you have tried clapping, you can repeat the experiment as many times as you like, making louder or softer sounds each time. Try banging on a drum or trashcan lid (right), and compare how far the light moves. You can also try singing or talking. Sing while holding your mouth close to the can and then far away.

You can then draw up a table of results, listing how far the light moved for each sound. Organize your table so that the quietest sound comes at the top of the table and the loudest sound at the bottom. Or, you could draw out your results as a bar graph. Use the vertical (y) axis to represent the number of squares the light moved and the horizontal (x) axis to represent the different sounds. You should find that the bars get taller as the sounds got louder. The louder sounds made the light move more than the quieter sounds—they had more energy.

Waves on a slinky

Although you cannot see sound waves in the air, you can see both transverse (up-and-down) waves, and compression (back-and-forth) waves using a slinky.

Find a smooth, open space outside—a playground works well. Tape down one end of the slinky with duct tape, or ask someone to hold onto it. Grab hold of the other end of the slinky, and stretch it out in a straight line. Move your hand up and down once. A transverse

wave will shoot along the slinky. Note that the wave moves sideways and at right angles to the way your hand moves. Next, give the slinky a sudden, quick push along its length. You should see a compression wave (a bunched up area of the springs) move along the slinky. Try pushing harder and softer, and notice how the compression wave changes.

You can see how a sound wave travels by pushing the end of a stretched-out slinky.

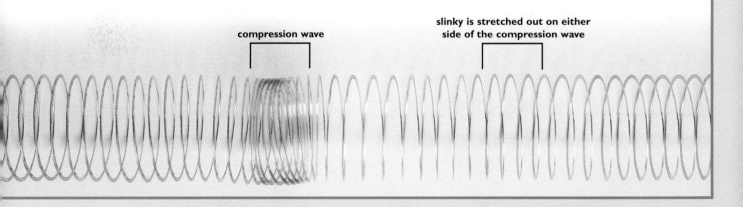

compression wave

slinky is stretched out on either side of the compression wave

ANALYSIS
Sound waves

When you make a noise near the can—whether it is clapping, banging on a trashcan lid, or singing—sound will travel out from the source of the noise as a compression wave. The sound energy makes each particle of air crash into the next one, passing on energy as it moves. It is a sound wave, and it spreads out from the source of the sound. When one of these sound waves reaches the rubber balloon, the rubber absorbs some of the energy by stretching and moving very slightly. As the balloon stretches, the mirror moves. This movement is very small and hard to see, so we shine a flashlight on the mirror to make the movement easier to see.

If you make a louder noise, you generate more sound energy. The particles of air will now crash into one another with more force, passing on more energy than before. When they reach the sound detector, these energetic waves hit the rubber harder than they did before and make it stretch farther. This, in turn, moves the mirror farther and pushes the light farther across the grid.

The sound detector is similar to your eardrum. Inside your ear is a very thin tissue. Sound waves strike this tissue, making it move. This movement is picked up by nerves in your ear canal, which send signals to your brain. Your brain interprets the signals as sounds.

The crack of a whip

A whip moves in a wave motion. The tip of the whip is pushed by the waves that move along the length of the whip. This creates a shock wave—a wave of air is pushed in front of the tip of the whip.

When the end of the whip travels faster than the sound waves produced by the motion of the whip, we hear a loud crack. It means that the tip of the whip reaches a point where it is moving faster than the speed of sound. As the tip of the whip breaks through the shock wave—the sound barrier—the sudden release of pressure makes a cracking noise. This loud noise is called a sonic boom.

The change in pressure as the tip of the whip breaks through the shock wave is small—similar to the pressure change you feel when you drop a few floors in an elevator. Because the change happens very quickly, you hear a boom.

The whip was actually the first human-made object to move faster than the speed of sound. The crack of a rifle is also caused by the bullet breaking the sound barrier.

ACTIVITY 2
SOUND ALL AROUND

If you close your eyes and listen carefully, you can build up a sound "picture" of the world around you. Your two ears help you pinpoint where sounds are coming from. You can explore this by building a simple sound locator.

Why do humans and other animals have two eyes and two ears? One reason is that having two eyes allows us to see the world in three dimensions, and having two ears allows us to "hear" the world in three dimensions. In other words, we can figure out where sounds are coming from and how they are moving around us.

FINDING SOUNDS

Suppose you are standing on a busy street with the noise of traffic streaming past you. Even with your eyes closed, you can still tell roughly where different sounds are coming from and in which direction the traffic is moving. Sound from a passing automo-

● *There is a speaker on either side of this concert stage. Each speaker plays the sound picked up from a separate microphone. That is called stereo sound.*

bile travels out in waves to your two ears. When the vehicle is on your left, the sound waves reach your left ear slightly faster than they reach your right ear. Because the sounds reaching your two ears are the same, your brain knows they are made by a single object. Since the sound waves reach your left ear first, your brain figures out that the object must be closer to your left ear than to your right. As the vehicle moves, your brain constantly compares the sounds reaching your two ears and figures out the vehicle's new position.

Having two ears also adds to our enjoyment of music. Our two ears are excellent at picking up sounds from different sources. Sound engineers, who re-create sounds in the movies, at concerts, and on CDs, aim to make sounds appear to come from all around us, just as in real life. American inventor Thomas Edison was the first man to record and play back sound. In 1877 he played a tinny version of "Mary Had a Little Lamb" on a phonograph. Since then the quality of recorded sound has been getting better and better.

MONO AND STEREO SOUND

Small radios that have just one loud-speaker sound flat and lifeless. Sound produced in this way is called monophonic (or mono). *Mono* means "one," and *phonic* means "hearing," so *monophonic* means "one-way hearing." Your ears hear the same sound coming from a single loudspeaker.

More sophisticated radios, hi-fis, and portable stereos have two speakers or two earphones, and they are called stereophonic (or stereo). The two speakers play slightly different sounds, and each of your ears receives a different sound "picture." If you have a portable stereo, try listening to a song and then switching the two headphones. The song will sound different when you do that—an instrument or voice that came from the right will switch to the left. When your brain hears stereo sound, it builds up a three-dimensional sound picture in your head. At its best, stereo can reproduce the sound that you would hear in a concert hall as if you were sitting in front of your favorite band as they play just for you!

SEEING WITH SOUND

Sound offers a useful way of "seeing" things when our eyesight is unable to do the job. Ships sometimes use foghorns to help them avoid dangerous coastlines in poor visibility. A ship's captain sounds the foghorn, and then listens for an echo bouncing back off the cliffs. The direction of the echo and the time it takes to return give a rough idea where the ship is in relation to the coast. Bats find their way around at night in a similar way by listening to echoes (see box on page 17). Your ears aren't as sensitive as a bat's, but they are still very good at locating sounds. In the activity on the following pages you can build a simple sound locator and compare it with your ears.

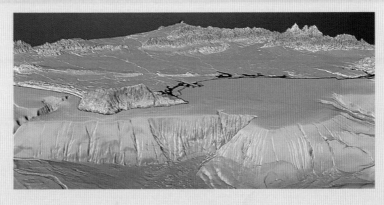

Seeing with sonar

Light travels poorly in seawater, so ships and submarines "see through the sea" with instruments that use sound instead. Fishing trawlers, for example, use a sounding device called sonar to figure out where shoals of fish are located and even what type of fish they are. Sonar takes its name from SOund Navigation And Ranging. It is also used to measure the depth of the sea and build up a picture of the seafloor (see picture below). Sonar works by transmitting bursts of sound and measuring how long the echoes take to bounce back off an obstacle. Sonar was originally invented in 1915 to help ships at sea avoid icebergs. This followed the sinking of the *Titanic* in 1912, when the ship hit an iceberg and sank to the bottom of the Atlantic Ocean, killing 1,515 people.

ACTIVITY

Spot that Sound

Goals

1. **Build a simple sound locator.**
2. **Test how useful it is for locating sounds.**

What you will need:

- 4 plastic funnels
- 2 pieces of flexible tubing, each about 4 feet (1.2m) long
- scissors
- tape
- ruler or piece of wooden dowel about 3 feet (1m) long
- modeling clay
- stool or chair
- blindfold
- alarm clock, radio, or other sound source
- a friend to help you

1 Attach one funnel to each end of the two pieces of tubing.

2 Tape one funnel from each piece of tubing to each end of the ruler.

3 Place a piece of modeling clay on the stool, and push the ruler into the clay to hold it in place.

Hearing aids

Before electronic hearing aids were invented, people with poor hearing used large "ear trumpets" that they held to their ears. They were similar to your funnels. They gathered sounds and made them louder. Try this yourself by cupping your open palms behind your ears. You should be able to hear faint sounds more clearly.

4 Ask a friend to help you. Put on the blindfold, and hold the two free funnels to your ears. Your friend will hold the sound source (here, an alarm clock). He or she can also record the results in a notebook.

Surround sound

Action movies use "surround sound" to make them seem more realistic. Loudspeakers positioned all around the movie theater can make sounds appear to come from anywhere, even behind the audience. It is surround sound that makes spaceships sound as if they are screaming overhead or ghostly footsteps sound as if they are creeping up on you from behind!

5 Your friend should choose somewhere in the room and set off the alarm clock. Keep the blindfold on, and try to figure out where the sound is coming from. When you think you know, point toward the sound.

6 Repeat the activity several times. Ask your friend to keep a note of where each sound came from and whether or not you correctly located the sound.

FOLLOW-UP   Spot that sound

When you have finished this activity, you should have an idea of how well you can find sounds with the locator. The way to find out how effective the sound locator is at locating sounds is to do a few more experiments and compare the results. Make up a table with four columns, like the one on the right, and fill in the results you got using the funnel sound locator. Try repeating the experiment, but this

	location	with locator	with only one funnel	without locator
1st trial	left corner of room, 10 feet from left funnel	did not point to sound	did not point to sound	pointed very close to sound
2nd trial	2 feet in front of right funnel			
3rd trial				
4th trial				

▢ You can record your results in a table like this one. That will make it easier to determine which method is best for locating the direction sounds are coming from.

time use only one set of funnels instead of both. Keeping your blindfold on, put a funnel to one ear, and cover up the other ear with your free hand. Repeat the activity, and record the results.

Now repeat the experiment without using the funnel sound locator at all. Point to where each sound is coming from using just your ears. Record your results in a table, as before.

▢ Can you locate sounds better using one funnel or two? Think about why we have two ears and how sound waves travel to our ears. Two funnels are better than one.

ANALYSIS
Sound all around

You should have found that the funnel locator was very good at making quiet sounds seem louder, but not as good at detecting sound direction as your ears. Using two ears is always more accurate than just using one ear, whether or not you use the funnel locator.

Why were your ears better at locating sounds than the locator? The outer flaps of your ears (each one is called a pinna, and together they are called pinnae) have many twists and ridges. The pinnae collect sounds just like the funnels of the locator, but the twists and ridges also change the sounds in various ways. From the way the sounds are changed, your brain can figure out more accurately where different sounds are coming from. When you use the funnel locator, sounds go directly into your ear without hitting the pinnae. That means your brain has less information, so it cannot locate the sounds as accurately.

Your brain normally figures out where a sound is by comparing the signals coming from both ears. When you use just one ear, either

An old-fashioned ear trumpet amplifies sounds. Modern electronic hearing aids are more sensitive and better at locating sounds. They tuck behind the ear.

with or without the locator, your brain finds it very difficult to locate a sound.

CONTROL EXPERIMENTS

Scientists normally perform at least two experiments before they compare sets of results. By changing only one thing at a time, they can study how each change affects the results. An experiment where nothing is changed is called a control. In this activity the control experiment involved pinpointing sounds using just your ears. You compared it with using the funnel locator and with covering one ear.

Flying by echolocation

Bats are amazing animals. Not only are they the only flying mammals, but they use a type of sonar called echolocation to find their food. Bats send out very high-pitched sound waves and listen for the echoes. Big echoes are obstacles to avoid; small echoes are insects to eat. Bats can identify the size, shape, and texture of an object by the echo. They are so sensitive to these echoes, they can distinguish individual hairs and fast-moving insects as small as gnats. Echolocation also allows bats to find their way around in the dark at night—that is when they are up and about, flying around and hunting for food.

ACTIVITY 3
SPEED OF SOUND

Sound travels much more slowly than light. People have built airplanes that can travel six-and-a-half times faster than the speed of sound. Traveling faster than the speed of sound is called breaking the sound barrier.

Light and sound are both waves. If you have ever watched a thunderstorm from a distance, you probably noticed how the flash of lightning seems to happen a few seconds before the clap of thunder. The thunder and lightning both happen at about the same time; but light moves much faster than sound, so you see the lightning before you hear the thunder.

Light travels at 186,000 miles per second (300,000 kilometers per second). The speed of sound in air is about 769 miles per hour (1,238 km/h). The fastest jet plane travels more than six-and-a-half times faster than the speed of sound.

You may have also noticed that you see a jet plane overhead before you hear the noise it makes. That is because it is traveling faster than the speed of sound—it is leaving its own sound behind.

The speed of sound is sometimes called the sound barrier. When a plane "breaks the sound barrier" by traveling faster than the speed of sound, it creates a loud noise called a sonic boom. It is caused by huge pressure disturbances around the plane called shock waves.

Sound does not always travel at the same speed. Through air its speed depends on the temperature and humidity (moisture content) of the air. With

Chuck Yeager (right) was the first person to fly faster than the speed of sound. Here he is being congratulated by the president of Bell Aircraft, the maker of his plane.

every degree Fahrenheit increase in temperature the speed of sound in air increases by more than 1 foot (30cm) per second. The speed of sound also increases with the humidity of the air. On humid days sound travels slightly faster than on dry days.

Sound also travels at different speeds in different materials. It usually travels much faster in liquids and solids than in gases, such as air. The speed of sound in water is typically about four to five times faster than in air, and it is faster in warmer than in colder water. Sound travels even faster in solids. In metals such as copper and steel the speed of sound

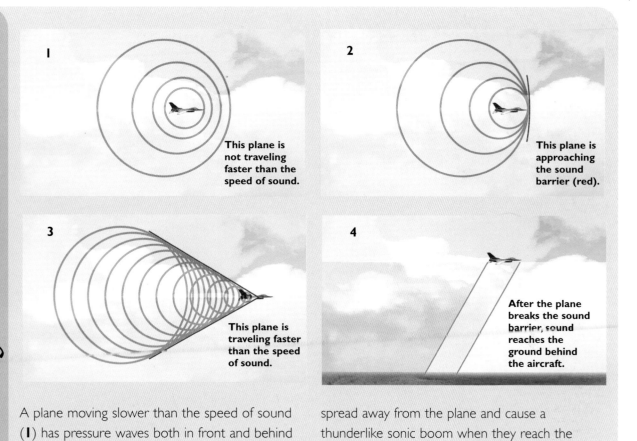

Breaking the sound barrier

1 — This plane is not traveling faster than the speed of sound.

2 — This plane is approaching the sound barrier (red).

3 — This plane is traveling faster than the speed of sound.

4 — After the plane breaks the sound barrier, sound reaches the ground behind the aircraft.

A plane moving slower than the speed of sound (1) has pressure waves both in front and behind it. As the plane reaches the speed of sound, Mach 1 (2), it catches up with its own pressure wave. The air piles up into a shock wave. At this point the plane vibrates violently. The shock waves spread away from the plane and cause a thunderlike sonic boom when they reach the ground (3). After the plane is going faster than Mach 1 (4) its flight is smooth because the waves fall behind the plane—the plane is moving faster than the pressure wave it produces.

is around 10–15 times faster than in air. The speed at which sound travels through steel is about 16,405 feet per second (5,000 meters per second).

Sound travels quickly, and over much greater distances, through water than through air. That is one reason why ocean animals such as whales use sound to communicate with one another. For this reason oceanographers (scientists who study the ocean) often use sound to make measurements under water.

We can tell many different things about the ocean using sound. Ships on the surface can check the depth of the sea using a device called an echo sounder. It sends pulses of sound down to the seabed, and times how long the echo (the sound bouncing off the seabed) takes to return. Because the echo sounder knows the speed of sound in water, it can calculate the depth of the ocean by multiplying the speed of sound by the time taken for the sound to travel that distance. Oceanographers also use sound to measure the nature of the rocks and other materials under the seabed, to listen to the way waves break on the surface, and even to measure the temperature of the ocean.

Humpback whales "sing" when they swim. The songs can last more than half an hour without repeating and are unique for each whale.

Measuring Sound

Goals

1. **Measure the speed of sound.**
2. **Calculate the speed of sound yourself.**

What you will need:

- *measuring tape*
- *a wall outside with a large empty space around it*
- *chalk*
- *trashcan lid*
- *spoon*
- *stopwatch*

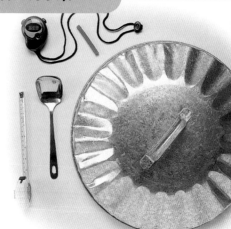

Accurate experiments

In this experiment you measure the time it takes sound to travel to the wall and back 20 times. You could just measure the time between a single clap and a single echo. But by making a much longer measurement, any delays you make in starting or stopping the watch will be a much smaller proportion of the time you measure. That makes your experiment much more accurate.

1 Measure a distance of 150 feet (50m) from the wall. Measure the distance as accurately as you can, and try to make sure you remain at a right angle to the wall. Mark the distance on the ground with chalk.

Go back to the wall, and measure 150 feet (50m) again from the same place as before. Mark the distance on the floor again.

If the two measurements of 150 feet (50m) are not exactly the same, draw a line halfway between them. By measuring the distance twice in this way, you make a much more accurate measurement than just measuring it once.

2 Both people should stand next to each other on the chalk mark, facing the wall. One person starts the stopwatch at the same time as the other person makes a sharp noise by banging on the trashcan lid.

3 When you hear the echo of the noise, make another noise with the sound generator so the clap and the echo occur at the same time. Repeat this 20 times. After you have clapped for the twentieth time, listen for the twentieth echo. When you hear it, immediately stop the watch, and record the new time in minutes and seconds. Write down the total time taken for the experiment.

Measuring up

The first person to measure the speed of sound in air was French mathematician Marin Mersenne (1588–1648). In 1640 he figured out that sound travels at 1,000 feet per second (300m/s), which is close to the value of 1,128 feet per second (344m/s) that scientists accept as the speed of sound today.

FOLLOW-UP ⟨ **Measuring sound** ⟩

In this experiment you measured the time it took sound waves to travel from you to the wall and back (300 feet) 20 times. The total distance traveled is 300 × 20, or 6,000 feet (2,000m). Speed equals the distance divided by the time, so to find the speed of sound, simply divide the total distance (6,000 feet) by the total time, in seconds, that you measured. Your answer will be in feet per seconds.

How does your measurement for the speed of sound compare with the generally accepted speed of about 1,128 feet per second (344m/s)? You may find your result is close to this figure, but it is unlikely to be exactly the same. Differences in air temperature and moisture affect the speed of sound and might make your value different from 1,128 feet per second.

Because you calculated the speed by taking two measurements, there are two other reasons why your measurement might not be what you expected. You might have measured either the distance or the time incorrectly.

Scientists often repeat their experiments several times and take an average of all their results to improve accuracy.

You could also repeat the experiment by standing different distances from the wall, by carrying out the experiment in other places, or by getting your friends to make the measurement instead of making it yourself. Once you have made several measurements of the speed of sound, take an average of them by adding the measurements together and dividing by the number of measurements. (For example, if you make three separate measurements, add them together, and divide by three.)

$$speed = \frac{distance}{time}$$

How temperature and moisture affect the speed of sound

Try the same experiment on a much hotter day and a much cooler day. You could measure the temperature on each day you do the experiment, and then plot a graph of the speed of sound (on the vertical, or y, axis) against the temperature (on the horizontal, or x, axis). You should find that the speed of sound increases as the temperature increases. You could also try measuring the speed of sound when there is a lot of humidity in the air (just after a rainstorm, for example).

◼ *Since sound waves bounce off a wall, you can measure the time it takes the waves to return to their starting point. That will give you the speed of sound.*

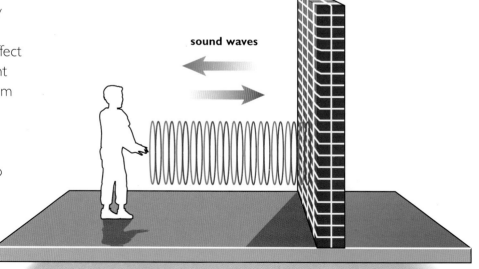

sound waves

ANALYSIS
Speed of sound

The standard accepted speed of sound is 1,128 feet per second (344m/s), which is 769 miles per hour (1,238km/h). After doing this experiment, you have probably realized that the speed of sound varies a great deal. Your results may have differed from 1,128 feet per second because the speed of sound changes.

How far off is that storm?

Now that you know sound travels at about 1,128 feet per second (344m/s), you can use this to figure out how far away a storm is. The next time there is a thunderstorm, look out of the window. As soon as you see a lightning bolt, start your stopwatch. Stop counting when you hear the thunder.

Light travels so quickly it seems to pass from the lightning bolt to your eyes instantaneously—it moves too fast for you to measure. Sound takes much longer to travel the same distance. The time you counted is the time it took for sound to travel from the lightning bolt to your ears. Let's say that the time you counted between seeing the lightning and hearing the thunder was five seconds. You know the speed of sound is 1,128 feet per second (344m/s). The distance to the lightning bolt is speed × time, or 1,128 feet per second (344m/s) × 5 seconds = 5,640 feet (a little more than 1 mile).

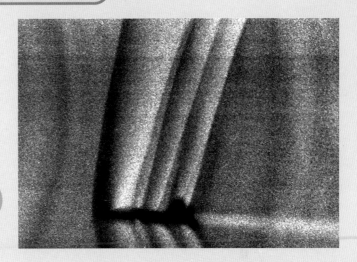

🔲 *This photo, taken with a special process called Schlerien photography, makes an image of sound waves, just as a jet breaks through the sound barrier.*

Sound, whether it is loud or quiet, travels at a constant speed, but this speed can change depending on certain conditions. For example, the speed of sound increases as temperature increases. At 70 °F (21 °C) sound travels through air at 1,128 feet per second (344m/s). But at 40,000 feet (12,192m), where supersonic jets fly, it is very cold, and the speed of sound is only 657 miles (1,060km) per hour. If you performed this experiment on a cool day, then you may have gotten a result lower than 1,128 feet per second.

The speed of sound through air also varies depending on the moisture content of the air. If there is a lot of moisture in the air, as on a humid or rainy day, sound will travel faster than on a dry day. If you performed this experiment on a humid or rainy day, you might have gotten a result higher than 1,128 feet per second for the speed of sound.

Your results will also be affected by your reaction time—how fast you clicked on the stopwatch. That is because there is always some delay between the time you hear a noise and the time you react to it.

ACTIVITY 4
RESONANT FREQUENCY

All objects can be made to vibrate at a particular rate called their resonant frequency. This vibration is the secret that lets most musical instruments work and can even explain why some bridges fall down.

Wet your finger, and then run it around the rim of a large and then a small wine glass. As your finger moves around the rim, the glass vibrates and makes a sound. You should find that the large glass vibrates slower and so makes a low musical note, while the smaller glass vibrates quicker, making a higher-pitched note.

RESONANCE

The rate at which something vibrates is called its frequency, and like the wine glasses, all objects have a particular frequency at which they naturally

🔵 *The opera singer Jessye Norman has trained her voice over many years. This training could make her voice powerful enough to shatter a wineglass.*

tend to vibrate. It is called their natural or resonant frequency. Opera singers can sometimes shatter a glass by holding notes at a certain pitch. As they sing near the glass's resonant frequency, the glass is bathed in the energy coming from the singer's voice. If the energy is close enough to the glass's resonant frequency, the glass picks up the energy, and starts to vibrate and make a singing noise. Exactly the same thing happened when you ran your finger around the rim of the glass. If the singer holds the note, the glass vibrates more and more powerfully until the vibrations are so strong that the glass shatters completely.

MAKING INSTRUMENTS SING

Most musical instruments use resonance to produce their sound. Percussion instruments vibrate at their resonant frequency when you hit them. Drums just seem to make a dull noise when you hit them, not a musical note. But if you listen to the drums in a symphony orchestra, you will notice there are many different drums, all tuned to produce notes of a different frequency. Xylophones, vibraphones, and marimbas have blocks of different sizes that produce notes of different pitch as you hit them. Each of these blocks has a different resonant frequency. Even the simplest percussion instrument of all, the triangle, has its own resonant frequency.

Other types of instruments use resonance in different ways. We will look at how string instruments work in Activity 6 (pages 34–39).

STANDING WAVES

Recorders, clarinets, flutes, and organs make noises when sound waves vibrate inside their hollow pipes. You can see how they work by taking an empty glass bottle and blowing across its neck. The bottle makes a musical note of a particular pitch

because you make the air inside it vibrate as you blow. But the air is not free to vibrate in any way it chooses. At the base, where the glass bottom seals the bottle completely, the air cannot vibrate at all. At the top, where the glass is completely open, the air can vibrate freely. A kind of frozen sound wave, called a standing wave, is created between the top of the bottle and the bottom. It has the shape of a quarter of a normal wave. Its narrowest point, where there is no vibration, is called a node and occurs at the bottom of the bottle. Its widest point, where there is maximum vibration, is called an antinode, and it occurs at the top of the bottle.

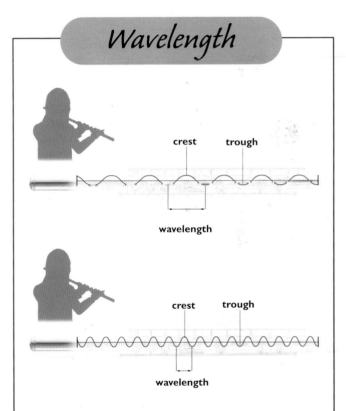

Wavelength

Like water waves, sound waves repeat themselves over and over again. Watch the waves on a beach, and you will notice that waves have crests (peaks) and troughs (hollows between the peaks), with regular spacing between the crests. This distance is called the wavelength. If a sound wave has a long wavelength, as in the wave from the flute in the top diagram, a low note is produced. If the crests are much closer together, as in the bottom diagram, then the note is much higher.

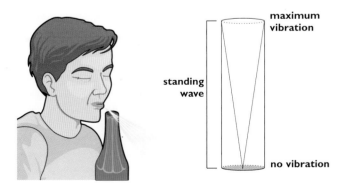

As you blow across a bottle, the air inside vibrates. It vibrates most at the open end, but not at the closed end, so one-quarter of a wavelength fits in the bottle.

Tuning Fork

Goals

1. **Measure the wavelength of sounds produced inside a hollow pipe.**
2. **See how the wavelength depends on the pitch of the fork.**

What you will need:

- *bucket about two-thirds full of water*
- *long plastic or cardboard tube (like those used to mail posters in) open at both ends*
- *tuning forks of several different pitches*
- *ruler and pen*

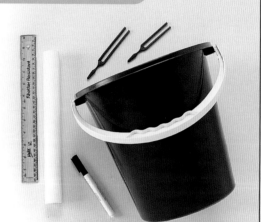

1 Put the tube into the water so it remains upright and is almost completely submerged. Strike one of the tuning forks on a table top and hold it, vibrating, over the end of the tube that is just poking up out of the water.

2 Listen carefully as you pull the tube up out of the water (keeping the fork held just above the tube opening). Keep listening until you find a point where the sound of the fork is at its loudest.

3 When you have found the point where the sound is the loudest, mark it with a pen.

Standing wave

When a standing wave is formed inside an open pipe, it is the size of one-quarter of a full wave. So the length of the full sound waves produced must be four times as long as the instrument.

4 Take the tube out of the water. Measure the distance from the mark to the top of the tube (the end that has not been in the water), and note the distance.

Troubleshooting

What if you don't hear any changes in the sound?

The change in volume may not be as loud as you might expect, so first try the experiment again in a quiet room, and listen very closely. If it still doesn't work, your tube may not be long enough, so try again with a longer tube.

Falling bridges

When people walk over a bridge or the wind blows against it, the bridge vibrates. If the vibration is at or near the bridge's resonant frequency, the bridge can vibrate so violently it tears itself apart. Resonance caused the collapse of the suspension bridge over the Tacoma Narrows in Washington State in 1940.

5 Put the tube back in the water, and keep moving it up and down until you find a second spot where the sound is at its loudest. Mark it with a pen, too.

6 Measure the distance from the second mark to the end of the tube, and record this distance. Now take a tuning fork of a different pitch, and repeat steps 1 to 4, recording the results each time.

FOLLOW-UP Tuning fork

Write up your results from the tuning fork activity on the previous page in a table like this one. Have a separate row for each tuning fork, and record the distances from the top of the tube to the loud spot in a column. Try repeating the experiment, but this time keep pulling the tube out of the water once you have found the first loud spot. Do you find any other loud spots? If you do, mark where they are on the tube. Then measure the distance from the open end of the tube to each spot, as you did before.
Record each new loud spot in a separate column.

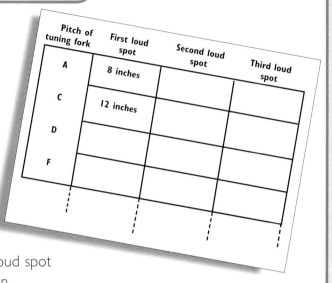

Pitch of tuning fork	First loud spot	Second loud spot	Third loud spot
A	8 inches		
C	12 inches		
D			
F			

ANALYSIS
Resonant frequency

The first point where the sound is at its loudest occurs when the tube vibrates at its resonant frequency, and a standing wave has been formed inside it. This standing wave has a node (point where the air doesn't move) where the tube is closed off by the water and an antinode (where the air moves most) at its open end (column 1, right). It lets a quarter of a wave form inside the tube, so the wavelength of the entire standing wave is four times the distance that you measured. Work through your table, multiplying the distance in the first column by four. The numbers you get are the wavelengths for each of the different tuning forks. You should find that the wavelength gets smaller as the pitch of the tuning fork gets higher.

Other standing waves can also form in the tube. A second wave will occur when three-quarters of a wave fits in the tube (column 2, right) and a third when there are five quarter wavelengths in the tube (column 3, right). Any other loud spots you found will be due to these

other waves. Multiply the distances in the second and third columns by $1\frac{1}{3}$ (1.3) and $\frac{4}{5}$ (0.8) respectively to calculate the wavelength—these numbers should be roughly the same for each tuning fork.

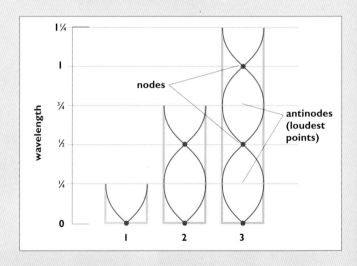

■ *A pipe open at one end can support several different standing waves, depending on its length. One-quarter, three-quarter, and five-quarter waves are shown.*

ACTIVITY 5
TRAVELING SOUND

When the speed of a sound wave changes, its direction usually changes, too. Like light waves, sound waves can be reflected, so it is possible to make "lenses" and "mirrors" for sound.

You might have noticed that if you hold a stick so that it is half in and half out of water, it appears to bend at the point where the water and air meet. That is because light travels at different speeds in air and water. Light waves travel more slowly through water than they do through air. The difference in speed makes the light waves bend (refract) as they pass from water to air, making the stick appear crooked.

During World War II (1939–1945), before radar was invented, batteries of sound detectors scanned the skies to warn of approaching aircraft. The funnels on each detector were shaped to collect distant sound waves.

Like light waves, sound waves also travel at different speeds in different materials. Sound waves travel faster through liquids and solids than through air. They also travel faster through warm air than through cold air.

Sound waves bend when they move from one substance to another substance where their speed is different. They bend when they travel from water to air, for example, or when they pass from air that is warm to air that is cool.

This change of speed according to temperature explains why it is often easier to hear sounds at night than during the day. At night air near the ground is often colder than air higher up. Sound travels more slowly in the colder, lower-lying air

and faster in the warmer air higher up. This difference makes sound waves bend down toward the ground, so sounds that are far away can be heard over a greater distance.

During the daytime a layer of warmer air may form near the ground. If so, sound waves near the ground will travel faster than sound waves higher up and so will bend upward, away from anyone listening. This means that, at ground level, sounds can be heard over greater distances at night, when the air is cooler, than during the day.

Sound through a Balloon

Goals

1. **Slow down sound waves.**
2. **Explore how sound waves travel through different gases.**

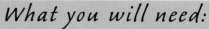

What you will need:

- *plastic bottle with a narrow neck*
- *funnel*
- *spoon*
- *2 tablespoons of baking powder*
- *vinegar*
- *balloon*
- *string and tape*
- *saucer*
- *radio*

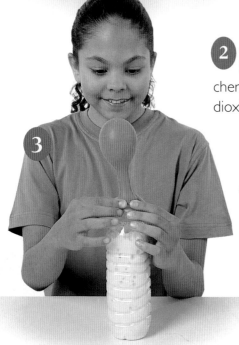

1 Using the funnel, put two tablespoons of baking powder into the plastic bottle.

2 Add some vinegar. You might hear or see fizzing as a chemical reaction forms carbon dioxide gas.

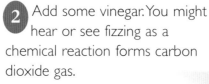

3 Quickly stretch the balloon over the neck of the bottle. It will begin to inflate as the carbon dioxide gas enters.

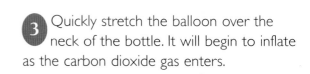

4 When the balloon is fully inflated, tie the neck securely, or tape it closed.

5 Attach the balloon firmly onto the saucer with tape so that it does not move.

6 Put the radio on a table about 1½ feet (50cm) from the balloon, and switch it on. Make it quite loud. Put your ear to the other side of the balloon, and move your head around until you find the point where the sound is loudest. Turn down the radio until you can barely hear it. If you cannot reach, ask a friend to turn it down while you listen.

Sound under water

The effects of helium on sound can be heard by divers. They breathe a mixture of oxygen and helium instead of ordinary air, which is mostly a mixture of oxygen and nitrogen. It keeps them from getting the painful condition called the bends when they come to the surface. But in this atmosphere the divers speak with comically squeaky voices.

7 Now take away the balloon. Does the radio sound louder or quieter?

FOLLOW-UP Sound through a balloon

This experiment works because the balloon is filled with a gas that is different from the surrounding air. You could go to a toy store and buy a balloon filled with helium, a very light gas. Helium-filled balloons float away because the helium is lighter than air. Try the experiment again using the helium balloon, and compare your results. You can also try these follow-up experiments without buying a helium-filled balloon.

Follow-up 1

Repeat the experiment, but instead of using the balloon filled with carbon dioxide, use another balloon that you have inflated using a bicycle pump (air from the pump will be less humid than your breath). This

time you should find the balloon makes little difference in the sound from the radio. Because the balloon and the surrounding air are essentially the same, the balloon makes no difference to the way the sound waves travel.

Follow-up 2

1. Repeat the original experiment with the carbon dioxide balloon, but this time move your head backward and forward until you find a place where the radio sounds loudest.
2. Measure the distance from the radio to the balloon and from the balloon to your head.
3. Write down both these figures in a table, as above.
4. Now move the radio closer to the balloon, and move your head backward and forward until you find the new loud spot.
5. Once again measure the distance from the radio to the balloon and from the balloon to your head.
6. Move the radio farther away

from the balloon than it was originally, and again find the new loud spot.
7. Once again measure the distance from the radio to the balloon and from the balloon to your head.

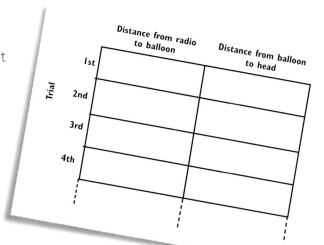

Trial	Distance from radio to balloon	Distance from balloon to head
1st		
2nd		
3rd		
4th		

8. Repeat this as many times as you wish, and then look at your results. How does the distance between the balloon and your head change as the distance between the radio and the balloon changes?

Follow-up 3

Go outside, in a busy area, with your carbon dioxide balloon and put it to one ear. Notice how you can hear distant sounds more clearly. The balloon is working as a sound telescope, focusing far-off sounds to make them louder at a point next to the balloon.

ANALYSIS

Traveling sound

When the gas-filled balloon was between your ear and the radio, you might have expected it to block off the sound waves. So you might have expected the sound to be louder when you removed the balloon. In reality you should have found that it was easier to hear the radio when the balloon was in place than when you removed it.

Although air contains a tiny amount of carbon dioxide, it consists mostly of nitrogen and oxygen. Molecules (tiny particles) of carbon dioxide are heavier than molecules of these other gases. Sound travels more slowly in carbon dioxide than in air because the molecules of carbon dioxide are heavier.

So, sound waves traveling through the balloon travel more slowly than waves traveling through the air next to the balloon. This makes the sound waves outside the balloon bend inward, much as light rays are bent inward by a

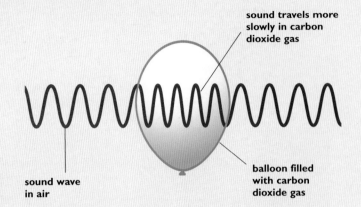

sound travels more slowly in carbon dioxide gas

sound wave in air

balloon filled with carbon dioxide gas

Sound waves slow down as they move through the carbon dioxide in the balloon, as shown by the closed-up waves in the diagram. Because of the difference in speed, the waves are bent inward and focused.

convex lens. (A convex lens is one that is thicker at the center than at the edges.) The balloon acts like a sound lens, focusing the sound and making it seem louder.

Amphitheaters

The theaters of the ancient world were often outdoors, but they were specially designed to make sure that everyone in the audience could clearly hear the words and music of the play. Called "amphitheaters," from the Greek word *amphi-*, meaning "around," they consisted of rising, circular tiers of seats. There was a clear line of sight between every spectator and the stage, so sound was not absorbed on its way to the listeners. The sides of the amphitheater were tilted so that all members of the audience were as close as possible to the stage. The loudness of the sound was strengthened by the fact that each person would hear sound reflected from the far side of the theater. This huge theater, in the Greek city of Epidaurus, was built in the 3rd century BC and could seat 14,000 people.

ACTIVITY 6
STRING SOUNDS

Sounds can be produced by making strings vibrate. The strings must be attached at both ends to keep them taut, and they can be plucked, hit, or rubbed to start a vibration.

In Activities 4 and 7 we can see how pipe instruments produce sounds when vibrating air particles make standing waves form inside their hollow bodies. String instruments, such as violins, guitars, harps, and pianos also make their sounds through standing waves.

When you pluck a guitar string roughly in the middle, waves of sound energy travel down the string in both directions, away from your finger. You can see the string vibrating as this happens. When the waves reach the points where the string is fastened at either end, they have nowhere to go. But energy cannot simply disappear. Just as ocean waves crashing against a sea wall are reflected back into the sea, so the

 Ravi Shankar playing the sitar, an instrument that has four main strings, and 13 additional strings.

energy waves on a guitar string travel back along the string in the direction they came from. When the two waves meet, they combine to form a standing wave. A musical pipe with an open and a closed end contains a standing wave that is one-quarter of a wavelength long. A guitar string is fixed at both ends, but can vibrate in the middle. This means the two ends of the string are nodes (minimum vibration), while the central point is an antinode (maximum vibration). The standing wave formed on a guitar string is thus one-half a wavelength long.

The standing wave on a guitar string makes the sound you can hear. It also makes the body of the instrument resonate, and that helps make the musical note sound louder.

PITCH AND FREQUENCY

String instruments bigger than a guitar, such as a cello or a double bass, have much longer strings. When longer strings vibrate, the standing waves they produce have a longer wavelength because the distance between the two fixed ends is greater. That means longer strings produce notes of a lower pitch.

Pitch is another way of describing how a musical note sounds. High notes (such as those sung by a young child) have a high pitch, while low notes (such as sung by an older man) have a low pitch. Another word for pitch is frequency. The frequency of any kind of a wave is equal to the number of vibrations that happen every second. It is the same as the number of peaks or troughs of the wave that move past a given point each second. If you stand on a pier and you can count three wave crests moving past

Every string on a harp is a different length, so they each produce sounds of different pitch.

each second, the frequency of the water waves is three complete waves per second. A complete wave is usually called a cycle, so the frequency is three cycles per second.

How guitars produce different notes

Guitars have either six or twelve strings, each of which produces a different note when you pluck it. The strings make different notes for two reasons: first, because they are slightly different thicknesses; and second, because they are tightened by different amounts by the pegs at the neck of the guitar. Sound waves travel faster down thinner and tighter strings, so the strings that make the

notes of higher pitch tend to be thinner, tighter, or both thinner and tighter than the strings that make the lower notes. Guitar notes increase in pitch as you move your finger down the fingerboard. By holding a string down, you shorten the standing wave formed when the string is plucked. That makes a standing wave of shorter wavelength and higher pitch.

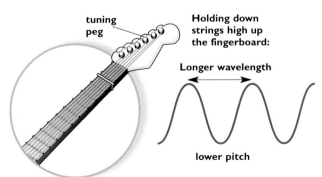

tuning peg

Holding down strings high up the fingerboard:

Longer wavelength

lower pitch

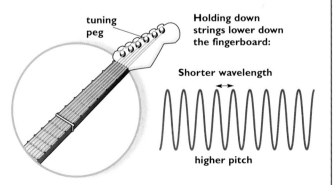

tuning peg

Holding down strings lower down the fingerboard:

Shorter wavelength

higher pitch

Make a String Instrument

Goals

1. Make a simple string instrument.
2. Investigate how the pitch of its note changes as you change the string's length and tightness.

What you will need:

- large, empty can
- hook
- modeling clay
- ruler
- elastic
- plastic bottle
- a set of weights, such as some identical metal nuts or identical coins

① Push or hammer the hook into the can, 1–2 inches (2.5–5cm) toward one side.

② Use modeling clay to attach the ruler to the opposite edge of the can so that it is standing on one of its long edges.

3 Cut a length of elastic, and tie one end around the nail. Tie the other end of the elastic to a small plastic bottle. Drop a few weights into the bottle, and hang it over the ruler. Place the tin at the edge of a table to make this easier.

4 Pluck the string of your instrument (the elastic) with your finger, and listen to the note that it makes.

5 Now try increasing the weight, and see what difference that makes to the note. Repeat this several times with different weights. If possible, add the same amount of extra weight each time. What do you notice about the way the note changes?

Troubleshooting

What if I can't get a good sound from the elastic?

You may find that thick elastic does not produce a clear twanging sound, like a guitar string. It you cannot find thin enough elastic, you can use a rubber band instead. Make sure that you stand back when you pluck the rubber band, in case the band breaks, or use eye protection. You can also try using thick string or twine.

FOLLOW-UP Make a string instrument

There are three follow-up experiments that you could try:

Follow-up 1

Insert a second hook into the can so it is closer to the ruler (perhaps half the distance between them), and repeat the experiment with the same elastic and the same weights. Notice how the pitch of the note changes.

Follow-up 2

Instead of using elastic, try using different elastic materials. You could try a rubber band, piano wire, or even an unwanted guitar or violin string. Before you start the experiment, figure out whether the material is more or less stretchy than the elastic. (You can do that by seeing how much it stretches when you hang weights from it.) How does that affect the notes produced by your instrument?

Follow-up 3

Attach elastic to the two different nails to make an instrument with two strings of different lengths. Hang a small weight from the shorter of the two pieces of elastic. Now, can you make roughly the same note with the longer of the two pieces of elastic? How many weights do you have to add to do that?

▶ *With two strings you can produce different notes or try to make the notes match, even though the strings are different lengths.*

ANALYSIS String sounds

The pitch (frequency) of sound that is made by a string depends on the length of the string, the tension (how much force pulls on the string), and the material the string is made of. Each of these different factors changes the way a standing wave is formed on the string and thus the pitch of the sound that is made.

You should have found that when you shortened the string, the pitch of the note increased. Generally, longer strings make lower notes than shorter strings, but that is not always the case. When you had the two strings of different lengths side by side, you should have found that you could make the same note on each string if you put more weight (to produce more tension) on the longer string than on the shorter one. The higher the tension on a string, the higher the pitch of the note that is formed. You may have found that you needed to increase the tension on the longer

A double bass has thicker strings that produce lower notes than other string instruments. A double bass also has a larger soundbox for a louder noise.

string quite a lot to produce the same pitch of note made by the shorter string. Musicians change the pitch of their strings by tightening or loosening them with the pegs at the neck end of the fingerboard.

Another way to change the pitch of the note is to change the material from which the string is made. Heavier materials generally make lower notes than lighter materials. You should have found that very thick rubber bands make lower notes than thinner ones.

Violins, for example, have four strings side by side. The two strings on the left, called G and D, make the lowest notes. They are typically made from metal and are thick. The two strings on the right, called A and E, make higher notes. They are thinner and may be made from a material called gut.

Vibrations, and therefore sounds, can be set up in strings by plucking (as in a harp, a guitar, and sometimes a cello), hitting (as in a piano), or rubbing (as in a cello and a violin).

Tuning instruments

String instruments are frequently out of tune because their strings are stretched to a high tension, and they work loose over time with the vibrations that happen when they are played. Changes in tension can make quite a difference in the pitch of the notes, and that is what makes the instrument sound out of tune. Tuning involves tightening the strings enough to produce the right notes. The notes made by a pipe instrument depend on the length of the instrument's tubelike body, which never varies, so tuning is not really a problem. Pianos are string instruments that make a noise when small hammers attached to the keys strike their strings. Tuning a piano is a skilled job that involves listening for beat sounds (see also Activity 8, pages 45–49).

A musician tunes his guitar by carefully tightening the strings with the tuning pegs.

ACTIVITY 7
WAVES IN OPEN PIPES

One way to produce a musical note is to make the air inside an open pipe vibrate in a particular way. Understanding how these pipes make their different notes explains how instruments such as flutes and trumpets work.

In Activity 4 (pages 24–28), we saw how a pipe that is open at one end makes sounds when standing waves are set up inside it. Pipes that are open at both ends can also make musical notes. In fact, most pipe instruments, from trumpets and saxophones to recorders and pan-pipes, work like this.

When a pipe is closed at one end and open at the other, the standing wave formed inside it has a node (point of minimum vibration) at the closed end because the air cannot move there. An antinode (point of maximum vibration) forms at the other end, where the air can move freely.

A pipe that is open at both ends makes a different kind of standing wave. Air at both ends can vibrate freely, so both ends of the pipe must be antinodes. This means the node must be at the center of the pipe. So, while a pipe open at only one end makes a

The sousaphone (above) was invented 150 years ago by John Philip Sousa for use in marching bands. It produces a low tone that helps keep the beat.

standing wave one-quarter of a wavelength long, a pipe open at both ends makes a standing wave one-half a wavelength.

VIBRATIONS IN PIPES

While stringed instruments make sounds using vibrating strings, pipe instruments make sounds by vibrating the column of air inside their hollow bodies. How this is done depends on the instrument. Wind instruments such as clarinets have a thin reed attached to their mouthpiece. When you blow into a clarinet, the reed vibrates, moving the air and creating standing waves inside the long, thin body of the instrument.

Other instruments, like trumpets, do not have reeds. Instead, trumpet players make their lips vibrate across the mouthpiece of the instrument. This vibration creates the standing wave and makes the musical notes.

Reed instruments

Wind instruments, like the clarinet, are open at both ends. A player blowing into a clarinet forces air across a reed. The reed vibrates the air inside the instrument, creating a standing wave. At the open ends of the clarinet are points called antinodes, where the air vibrates most. In the middle is a node, where no vibrations occur. This allows one-half a standing wave to form inside the clarinet.

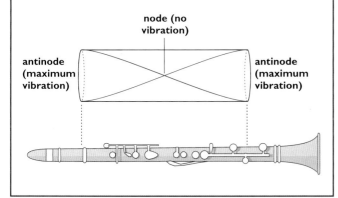

node (no vibration)

antinode (maximum vibration)

antinode (maximum vibration)

DIFFERENT STROKES, DIFFERENT NOTES

As we saw in Activity 6 (pages 34–39), the note produced by a string instrument is changed by altering the length of the string, either by having a longer or shorter instrument or by moving your fingers on the strings. In a pipe instrument the musical notes depend on the length of the air column. Longer wind instruments (such as clarinets) produce lower notes than shorter ones (such as recorders and piccolos). Most instruments have a method of changing the length of the air column to produce different notes. In a trombone a sound pipe slides in and out, changing the length of the air column and producing higher or lower notes. In saxophones keys on the side of the instrument open and close holes to change the length of the air column. If you play a recorder, you are using your fingers instead of keys to open and close the holes.

FREQUENCY AND WAVELENGTH IN PIPES

You may have already noticed that the pitch (frequency) of a sound is related to its wavelength. Think about a short wind instrument, such as the piccolo. The standing wave an instrument produces is related to the length of the instrument, so the short piccolo has a short wavelength. That makes the sounds it produces high-pitched. In a longer instrument, such as a bassoon, the standing waves have a longer wavelength and produce much lower sounds.

Short wavelengths produce high-pitched notes, and long wavelengths produce low-pitched notes. Because of this, frequency (pitch) and wavelength can be said to be the "opposite" of one another—as frequency goes up, wavelength goes down, and vice versa. Multiplying the frequency of a sound wave by its wavelength gives you the speed at which the wave travels.

Galileo Galilei

The Italian physicist and astronomer Galileo Galilei (1564–1642) was one of the first scientists to study sound properly. In one of his early experiments he moved a chisel over a brass plate that had ridges on it. The faster he moved the chisel over the ridges, the more vibrations it produced per second, and the higher the pitch of the sound it made. In this way he showed that frequency of sound (the number of vibrations per second) was related to pitch. After making many other studies, Galileo set out the basic ideas about sound that we still use today.

Straw Pipes

Goals

1. **Produce a standing wave in a pipe that is open at both ends.**

2. **See how the wavelength of the sound depends on the pipe's length.**

What you will need:

- *several drinking straws all the same length*
- *ruler*
- *pen*
- *a pair of scissors*
- *tape*
- *modeling clay (to use in the follow-up activity)*

1 Take one straw, and use the ruler to measure 1 inch (2.5cm) from one end. Draw a line on the straw to mark this point.

2 Cut the straw where you made the line, and throw the smaller piece away.

3 Now take more straws, and repeat steps one and two, each time cutting another inch up from the bottom, until you have six or seven straws, each differing in length by one inch.

4 Line the straws up in order of height, from longest to shortest, and then tape them all together to make your straw pipe.

4

Standing wave

In this activity you are making a simple pipe instrument out of drinking straws. There's nothing to keep you from adding as many pipes as you want, but you have a long way to go to match the world's biggest pipe instrument. That title belongs to the pipe organ at the Atlantic City Convention Hall in New Jersey. It contains an estimated 32,000 separate pipes. The largest pipe in the instrument is more than 64 feet (19.5m) long and 3 feet (1m) around at the top. The entire pipe was carved from a single tree!

5

5 Blow across the top of your pipe, and notice how the pitch changes as the straws get shorter or longer.

FOLLOW-UP Straw pipes

If you have a musical instrument, compare the notes made by your straw pipe to those made by your instrument. Try to identify which notes are made by which pipe. The notes made by your pipe may not be exactly the same as those of your instrument, but they may still be similiar enough for you to match them up.

Use small blobs of clay to seal off the ends of each pipe. Do the notes sound higher or lower in pitch this way?

You could also examine how notes change with the length of the straw in another way. Take a straw, measure its length, and divide it in half to find the midpoint. Cut half-way through the straw at its midpoint. Bend the straw at a right angle so that you open up the cut. Blow into one end of the straw, and listen to the note it makes. Cover the far end of the straw with your finger, and blow into the flattened end of the straw. Listen again to the musical note. How do they differ?

ANALYSIS
Waves in open pipes

The length of an open pipe is equal to half the wavelength of the sound it produces. So, to find the wavelength of the note, measure the length of each pipe, and then multiply the length of each pipe by two.

Using the figure you calculated for the speed of sound in Activity 3 (see pages 18–23), you can now work out the frequency of each note. If frequency × wavelength = speed of sound, frequency = speed of sound ÷ wavelength. So, the frequency of each note is the speed of sound divided by the wavelength. Remember that the speed of sound and wavelength must be in the same units (so use either feet, inches, or meters through the whole calculation).

Blowing across your pipe, you vibrate the air inside the open straws, creating standing waves. The longer the straw, the longer the wavelength of the standing wave that can fit

inside it. Because longer wavelengths produce lower frequencies (lower pitch) than shorter ones, you should notice that the longer straws produce the lower-frequency notes.

When you blew into the cut straw in the follow-up, air rushed along the first pipe and across the open end of the second pipe, which you bent at right angles to the first. This sets up a standing wave in the second tube, with an antinode at both ends and a node in the middle. That means the wave in the pipe is exactly half a wavelength long. When you cover the bottom end of the second pipe, air can no longer vibrate at the lower end. You now have a closed pipe with an antinode at the top and a node at the bottom. The standing wave is now a quarter of a wavelength long. The result is that the closed pipe produces a shorter wavelength (higher-pitched) note than when it is open.

BEAT SOUNDS

Listen to the sound from two very similar notes being played together, and you can hear how they join together to produce a regular rising and falling in volume called beats. In this activity you'll see how these beats come about.

If you have ever watched ocean waves crashing into a sea wall or cliff, you will have noticed how the waves tend to be reflected back into the sea. Very often an incoming wave meets a wave that has been reflected back from the sea wall, and the two collide. When that happens, the two waves add together to form a new wave. If the peaks of the incoming wave meet the troughs of the reflected wave, the two waves cancel each other out and disappear. If the peaks and troughs of the incoming wave match those of the reflected wave, however, the peaks and troughs can add together. This creates a new wave that has much bigger peaks and troughs than either of the original waves.

HOW BEATS ARE MADE

Exactly the same thing can happen with sound waves. Two sound waves that meet can cancel one another out if the peaks of one match the troughs of another. Alternatively, they can add together (reinforce one another) if the peaks and troughs of one match up with those of the other. If two sound waves with very slightly different frequency meet one another, something different happens. Their peaks and troughs can never exactly match up because the waves are of slightly different lengths. This causes the two waves to cancel out in some places and add together in others. The result is a new wave that is bigger in some places, but smaller in others, than either of the original waves.

The height of a wave (the vertical distance from the center of a trough to the top of a peak) is called its amplitude. For a sound wave the amplitude is the same thing as its loudness: the bigger the ampli-

You can see how different waves affect each other by watching the sea. Although these waves are water waves, sound waves behave in a similar way.

tude, the taller the wave, and the louder the sound. If two sound waves of slightly different frequency add together, they make a third wave whose amplitude gets bigger and smaller in a regular way. The result is a sound that seems to wax and wane, pulsing louder and softer over time. This regular pulsing of the volume is called beats.

Toot Together

ACTIVITY

Goals

1. **Add together two sounds of slightly different frequencies to produce beats.**

2. **See how the beat changes over time.**

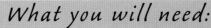

What you will need:

- *two swanee whistles (whistles with a movable piston that changes the sounds they make)*
- *1 foot (30cm) ruler*
- *stopwatch or wristwatch with a second hand*

1 Take one whistle for yourself, and give the other to your friend. Pull the piston of each whistle out halfway. Get your friend to blow into their whistle so that they keep playing the same note. Take your whistle, and move the piston until your note is exactly the same as your friend's.

2 Now pull the piston of your whistle out slowly. You should be able to hear the volume of the sound produced by the two whistles together rising and falling in beats. If you pull your piston even farther out (so the two notes differ even more), you should notice the changes in volume happen quicker and quicker until you can no longer hear them. What happens as you push the piston back in again?

3 Now, repeat step one, but this time measure the length of pistons sticking out from your whistles.

4 Slowly pull the piston out of your whistle until you begin to hear beats. Start the stopwatch when the beats are at their loudest point, and measure the time taken for ten beats.

5 Note down the time taken for the ten beats together with the distance that the piston is sticking out of your whistle

Troubleshooting

What if I can't hear any beats, or they are not regular?

For the beats to be regular, it is important that the two notes that join together to make them are regular, too. Make sure that you and your friend blow into your whistles with a steady and even breath, so that the notes that you make have a constant volume.

Tuning pianos

One practical use of beats is in tuning pianos. Each string in the instrument is compared with strings that produce notes of similar pitch. By listening for beats when two strings play at once, a skilled piano tuner can tell exactly how much each string needs adjusting.

6 Now, pull your piston a little farther out until you notice the beats have speeded up a little. Measure the time for ten beats, and note this down together with the distance that your piston is sticking out.

7 Keep repeating step 6 until you can no longer hear any beats in the sound.

FOLLOW-UP

Toot together

You should have found that you could hear beat sounds when the two whistles were playing notes of very slightly different pitch. As you increased the difference between the two notes, the beats should have sounded more quickly. As you made the two notes similar again, the beats should have slowed down and eventually disappeared.

Because you measured the timing of the beats together with the different lengths of the pistons that produced them, you will be able to see how the frequency of the notes and the timing of the beats are related.

To do this, plot a graph of the beat time (in seconds) on the y axis against the difference in piston length (in inches or centimeters), like the one shown here. You can work out the time for a beat by dividing the time you got for ten beats by ten (the reason for doing this is that it is much more accurate than just measuring one beat on its own). When you have plotted all the points that you recorded on the graph, see how they relate to each other—do they lie on a line or on a curve, or are they all spread out?

Beat time in seconds

40
30
20
10
0

0   1   2   3

Piston length in inches

ANALYSIS

Beat sounds

Although it makes a whistling noise, a swanee whistle is actually a type of pipe instrument that is closed at one end. As you saw in Activity 7 (see pages 40–44), the wavelength (and thus the pitch) of the note made by a pipe closed at one end depends on the length of the air column inside. The more you pull out the whistle's piston, the longer the air column, and the longer the wavelength of the standing wave inside. The longer the wavelength, the shorter the frequency, and the lower the note's pitch. That is why the whistle swoops down to a lower note when you pull out the piston.

When two whistles play together with their pistons pulled out by the same amount, they should both be playing the same note, with the same pitch, frequency, and wavelength. As the piston of one of the whistles is pulled out a little farther, the wavelength of the note produced gets longer, and so the note has a lower frequency and pitch. When two whistles with their pistons pulled out to slightly different lengths are played at the same time, they produce notes of two slightly different frequencies. These two notes mix together and produce the beats that you can hear as the pulsing change in volume.

The farther you pull out the piston on one of the whistles, the more the pitch and frequencies of the two notes differ, and the faster the beats become. When you plot a graph of the beat time against the change in piston length, you can see exactly how the change in piston length (and hence the difference in frequency and pitch of the two notes) affects the timing of the beats they produce.

If you look at the points on your graph, you should see that you can take a ruler and draw a straight line through them (don't worry if all the points do not fit exactly on a line; even professional scientists rarely measure things so well that their results are perfect!). The fact that

You can sometimes hear the engine noise from a helicopter with two rotors rising and falling because the noise from the two engines combines to produce beats.

the points all fit roughly on a straight line shows that the timing of the beats depends exactly on the difference in pitch between the two notes. If the points did not all fit on a straight line like this, and you found that they linked up in a curve or could not be easily joined up at all, it would show that the timing and difference in pitch either did not depend on each other at all, or that the way they related to each other was much more complicated.

Constructive and destructive interference

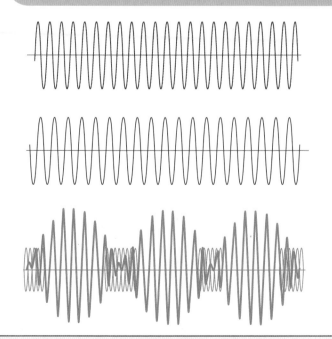

The diagrams opposite show how two waves can add together to produce beats. The frequencies of the red and blue waves are very similar, but they are not exactly the same. This means that their peaks and troughs line up in some places, but not in others. Where they line up, they add together and get bigger—that is called constructive interference. When the peak of one wave lines up with a trough of the other, then the waves cancel each other out, and there is no wave—that is called destructive interference. The green wave shows the result of the blue and red waves adding together. In parts it is bigger than either the red or blue waves, but in others it is smaller. In a sound wave you can hear that as a change in volume.

SOUND INSULATION

Hearing the wrong noise at the wrong time can be annoying or dangerously distracting, and excessively loud noise can be harmful to health. Sound engineers have to know how to block out unwanted sound.

We have already seen in Activity 3 (pages 18–23) that sound waves travel at different speeds in different materials. They travel much faster in solids, such as steel, than in liquids such as water. And they travel much faster in water than in air, the material through which we normally hear sound. The materials that carry sound fastest also carry it farthest. Sound can sometimes travel hundreds of miles through the oceans—much farther than the same sound would travel in air.

How far sound waves travel depends on many factors. A source of sound gives off energy, which spreads out in much the same way that heat energy

The roar of jets taking off and landing is a serious nuisance for people nearby. The noise can be reduced by better insulation of the engines and of buildings.

spreads out from a fire. The farther away from the sound source you get, the less energy reaches you in each second.

Sound waves, and thus sound energy, can also be reduced by the material the sound is traveling through. As the sound wave passes through a material, the molecules carrying the sound vibrate. As the molecules vibrate, some of the original sound energy is turned into heat and lost.

There are three main ways of dealing with unwanted sounds. The simplest method is to reduce the noise at the source. That might involve padding an engine to keep it from vibrating, or putting a noisy computer printer inside a special plastic cabinet that prevents sound from escaping. It is not always possible to contain sound in this way, however. Traffic noise is a good example of noise pollution that cannot be eliminated at its source.

Another method of reducing noise is to interrupt it on its journey from the source to the listener. Large mounds of earth called berms are often built beside highways. They are positioned to reflect traffic noise away from people's homes.

If sound cannot be reduced at the source or interrupted on its journey, the final way to reduce it is to surround listeners with sound-absorbing materials to prevent the noise from reaching them. Houses built near airports usually have very thick double-glazed, or even triple-glazed, windows to reduce noise. They consist of two or three panes of glass separated by wide air spaces. Such windows absorb sound very well.

A highway worker wears ear-protectors while he uses a pneumatic drill. Without this protection his hearing would probably be harmed by years of such work.

Sound waves can also be weakened when they are reflected—when they bounce back off a wall, for example. They are also weakened when they are refracted (bent). On a hot day, for example, sound waves bend upward into the atmosphere.

DEALING WITH UNWANTED SOUNDS

Unwanted sounds are often referred to as noise pollution. Everything from the roar of a jet plane to the noise of construction work, the sound of traffic, or music blasting out from a stereo can be described as noise pollution. Fortunately, some materials absorb unwanted sounds in the same way as a towel soaks up water. These materials can be incorporated into the design of buildings or built into special protective headgear called ear-protectors to control the movement of sounds.

Absorbing performance

A packed concert hall can sound very different from an empty one because people's bodies absorb sounds. That makes it difficult for the orchestra to produce the same sound in the performance that it achieved in the rehearsals. So the seats are usually covered with special fabrics to absorb sounds in the same way as a person's body. That way the hall sounds the same whether it is empty or full.

Muffling Sound

Goals

1. **Compare how well different materials work as sound insulators.**

2. **Learn how to reduce sound.**

What you will need:

- *small transistor radio*
- *variety of materials, such as cardboard, padded envelopes, rubber sheeting, and polystyrene*
- *tape*
- *cushion or pillow*
- *ruler*
- *scissors*

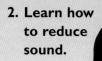

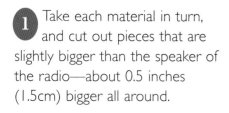

Soundproofing buildings

Construction engineers use several methods to insulate buildings from unwanted sounds. They make outer walls very heavy, because they do not allow sound through as readily as lighter walls do. They make windows of several layers of glass with spaces between. They install air-conditioning so that windows can be kept closed. They put insulating material in the walls, and they build double floors.

1 Take each material in turn, and cut out pieces that are slightly bigger than the speaker of the radio—about 0.5 inches (1.5cm) bigger all around.

2 It is important that you cover the speaker in the same way for each different material. You will need at least 0.5 inches (1.5cm) thickness of each material. For the thinner materials cut several pieces, and place them one on top of another until you have this thickness.

3 Put one of the materials over the radio's speaker. Rest the radio on the cushion or pillow so that stray sound coming from the back is absorbed. Turn the radio down very slowly until you can't hear the sound anymore. Read off the number from the volume scale, and write it down in a table next to the name of the material. If the radio doesn't have a volume scale, mark one with chalk, from 0 to 10.

4 Repeat the previous step with each of the materials in turn.

Killing sound

One amazing type of ear-protector actively destroys harmful sounds. Electronic circuits measure the unwanted sound and then generate "antisound" inside the earphones. The antisound is identical to the original sound except that its waves are out of step with the original waves. The waves of sound and antisound cancel each other out. The result is that the wearer of the earphones hears no sound at all.

FOLLOW-UP   Muffling sound

A more accurate way of carrying out this experiment is to measure the loudness of the radio's sound with a decibel meter. It is a scientific instrument for measuring noise levels. It shows the result in units called decibels (dB), the standard scientific units for the loudness of sounds. Rustling leaves measure about 20 dB, and an average noisy street measures about 70 dB.

Testing different materials

Here is an experiment you can try using the decibel meter.

1. Turn the radio up to a medium volume, and keep the volume control at this point with tape. Do this because it is important that you do not alter the volume from now on.
2. Place the decibel meter at a position where it shows a high reading for the sound from the radio. Then leave it there, and do not move either the radio or the meter.
3. From the decibel meter read the sound level (in dB) of the uncovered radio. Write this figure down.
4. Fasten each material in turn over the speaker, as before.
5. Instead of turning down the volume each time, read off the new sound level (in dB) from the decibel meter. Write this figure down in a table.

6. Repeat the experiment for each of the materials.

Different thicknesses

Using the decibel meter, you can do another experiment to study accurately what difference the thickness of insulation makes to the volume of sound.

1. Choose one material from your set that you found to be a fairly good sound insulator.
2. Cut out five or six pieces of this material of identical sizes.
3. Set up the radio as before, with the volume control taped at one setting.
4. Place the decibel meter in about the same position as before, so that it is showing a high reading. Then leave it there, and do not move either the radio or the meter once you have started the experiment.
5. Read the sound level (in dB) of the uncovered radio, and write this figure down in a table. The table should have a column headed "No. of layers of material" and another headed "dB." Put 0 in the first column and the decibel figure in the second.
6. Tape one layer of material over the radio speaker. Measure the new sound level from the

meter. Write 1 in the first column of your table, and put the sound level from the meter in the second column.
7. Add a second thickness of material, and measure the new sound level. Write down the sound level in your table for two layers of material.
8. Add the new layers of material one at a time, measuring the new sound levels and writing them down.
9. When you have finished, plot a graph of sound level (y axis) against the number of thicknesses of material (x axis).
10. What do you notice about the sound level as the thickness of insulation increases?

ANALYSIS

Sound insulation

Y ou should have found that increasing the thickness of a piece of material makes it a more effective sound insulator. As a sound wave travels through a material, it loses energy and becomes fainter.

You should also have found that some materials are better at blocking out the noise of the radio than others. The reasons why some materials are better sound insulators than others are complex, but in general, dense materials (such as rubber) absorb sound more strongly than less dense materials (such as paper). In addition, softer materials (such as plastic foam) are better than harder ones (such as cardboard).

One reason why foam absorbs sound strongly is that the sound is reflected again and again from the surfaces of the hundreds of thousands of bubbles in the foam. At every reflection the sound is weakened.

Musical instruments are tested in "dead rooms." Sound is repeatedly reflected by the foam covering the walls and partly absorbed at each reflection.

Softening the sound

Furniture in a room helps make it more comfortable for the ears as well as the body. The carpets, curtains, and soft furniture absorb some of the sounds in the room and reduce echoes (below left). This makes the sound from radio and TV sets less harsh and more pleasant to listen to. The room sounds very different when the furniture has been removed, as you will know if you have ever moved or helped decorate a room. The sound is absorbed less strongly, and so the sound waves bounce off the walls and floor, reaching the listener by several paths (below right), creating echoes.

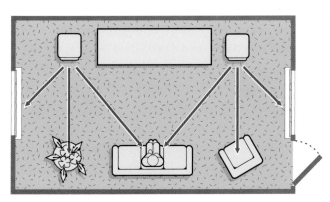

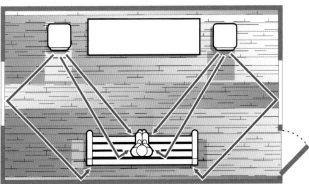

ACTIVITY 10
THE DOPPLER EFFECT

When an ambulance speeds along the street, the sound of the siren changes as the vehicle passes you. The sound drops to a lower pitch. That is called the Doppler effect, and you can explore it further in this activity.

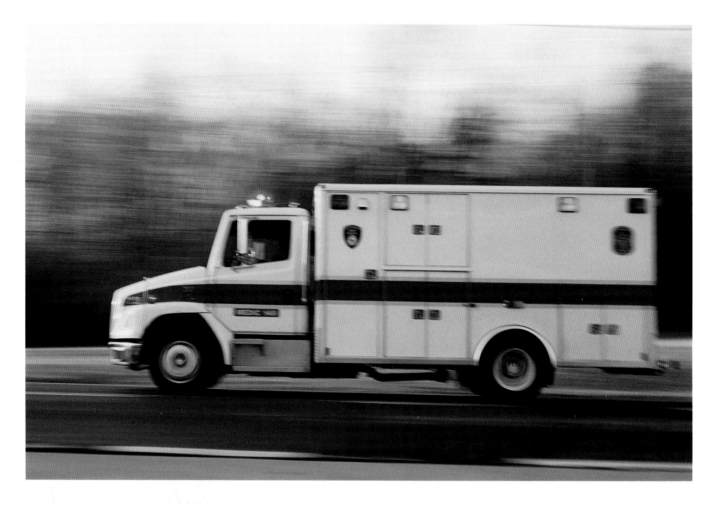

When an ambulance or fire truck drives past, the pitch of the siren seems to shift to a lower note. It sounds as if the driver has flipped a switch and turned down the pitch of the siren. This phenomenon is called the Doppler effect (or Doppler shift), and it is caused by the way the speed of the vehicle affects the sound waves traveling out from the siren.

Imagine you are a sound wave standing on the edge of the siren, about to leap out into the air. You have a certain frequency (how closely the sound

The blaring siren of an ambulance sounds much higher when the vehicle is racing toward you. As it passes and drives away, the sound has a lower note.

waves follow behind one another). You will shoot through the air at 1,128 feet per second (344 meters per second—the speed of sound in air) toward anyone who is listening, making the sound of the siren and finally reaching the inside of the listener's ears. The higher the frequency of the siren's sound, the higher the pitch will appear to the listener.

Suppose there is someone listening to the truck some distance ahead of it (person **A** in the diagram). The sound waves set out from the siren at 1,128 feet per second (344m/s). However, the truck itself is also moving forward at a certain speed—say, 60 miles per hour (100 feet per second, or 30m/s). That means the speed through the air of the sound wave is the speed of sound plus the speed of the truck, or 1,128 + 100 = 1,228 feet per second (375m/s).

If sound waves travel faster toward the listener, they will also seem to arrive more frequently. In other words, the pitch of the sound will seem to be higher. The truck's siren normally has a certain frequency and pitch. Frequency is measured in hertz (Hz). Let's say the truck's siren has a frequency of 1,000 Hz. If the truck is moving at 60 miles per hour (30m/s), this extra speed will make the siren sound as if it has a frequency of 1,100 Hz.

The reverse applies to a person who is standing behind the truck listening to it move away (person **C**). A sound wave setting off backward toward the listener will be slowed down a little by the speed of the truck. The waves' actual speed is the speed of sound minus the speed of the truck: 1,128 − 100 = 1,028 feet per second (314m/s). Sound waves travel more slowly toward the listener behind the truck, so they arrive less often and sound lower in pitch. To a listener behind the truck the 1,000 Hz siren will sound more like a siren of 920 Hz.

D is a firefighter on board the truck. No matter how fast the truck is moving, he or she hears no change in the siren's pitch.

As the truck pulls away from C, the siren's sound waves are stretched farther apart, making a lower note.

The truck races toward A. The siren's sound waves are pushed together, making a higher note.

As the fire truck races past B, he hears the siren appear to drop from a higher to a lower note. That is the Doppler effect.

🔲 *As a fire truck drives past, listeners A, B, C, and D each hear the fire truck's siren differently.*

If a third listener (person **B**) stands in between the other two listeners and listens as the truck passes by, he or she will notice the pitch of the siren shift suddenly from 1,100 Hz to 920 Hz—quite a considerable drop in pitch. Of course, the pitch of the siren only appears to change because of the position of the listeners; it really remains the same all the time. If you were a firefighter sitting on board the truck (person **D**), the siren would always sound the same pitch to you.

Speed cameras

Police speed guns are perhaps the best-known use of the Doppler effect. When a police officer standing by the roadside aims a radar gun at a speeding car, a tiny computer inside the gun uses the Doppler effect to calculate the car's speed. Radar waves (a type of radio wave) traveling out from the gun hit the car, and are reflected back toward the speed gun. The car's own speed increases the speed of the radar waves (if the car is driving toward the gun) or reduces them (if it is driving away). By working out how much the speed of the waves is changed, the computer calculates how fast the car is moving, and displays it on a digital readout.

Build a Bull-roarer

Goals

1. **Make a sound generator called a bull-roarer.**
2. **Use the bull-roarer to test the Doppler effect.**

What you will need:

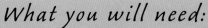

- a cardboard tube or a strip of thick cardboard made into a tube
- a length of thick string about 3 feet (1m) long
- blindfold
- a friend to help you

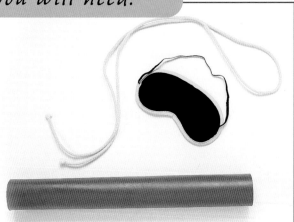

Safety tip

The forces acting on the bull-roarer increase the faster you swing it around. So make sure you tie the string very securely to the cardboard tube. Also, do this experiment outside so you don't damage or break anything. Be sure that you and your friend are standing a safe distance apart—remember that one of you is wearing a blindfold and could stray into the path of the bull-roarer!

1 Ask an adult to make two holes at one end of the tube. He or she could use a hole punch or scissors. Put the string through the holes, and tie it securely.

2 Now ask a friend to help you. You will operate the bull-roarer, and your friend is going to listen to the sound that it makes.

3 The two of you should stand about 30 feet (10m) apart. You should swing the bull-roarer around your head at a steady speed to make a note of continuous pitch. It is important that you make the same pitch of note throughout the experiment.

4 Your friend should be blindfolded, or have their eyes closed, and concentrate on the pitch of the note.

30 feet (10m)

5 Now, start to walk briskly along a straight line in front of your friend, taking care to make the same pitch of note with the bull-roarer (that is, to keep swinging it at a constant speed).

Your friend should listen carefully and try to spot the moment when you walk past him by listening for a shift in the pitch of the bull-roarer (the Doppler effect).

6 When you have done this, swap roles and places with your friend, and repeat the experiment.

Troubleshooting

What if my friend can't hear the Doppler effect?

Be sure to swing the bull-roarer at a constant speed throughout the activity. If you change the speed, the pitch of the note will vary, and you will be unable to pinpoint the Doppler effect. If you still have trouble hearing the Doppler effect, try swinging much more quickly. (That will make the Doppler effect more pronounced, and you should hear it more clearly.)

You could try using a different device to generate sound. It should make continuous loud notes at the same frequency. A pitch pipe (a small set of pipes used for tuning instruments) would work well. Or you could use a musical instrument such as a recorder and play one long note.

FOLLOW-UP Build a bull-roarer

There are a few more activities that you can try to help you understand the Doppler effect more fully.

Follow-up 1

Swing the bull-roarer around twice as quickly (or as quickly as you can), and see what effect that has on the Doppler effect that you hear. You should find that the shift in pitch is much more noticeable. Indeed, if you exactly double the frequency of the bull-roarer, you will find that the drop in pitch is twice as much as it was before.

Follow-up 2

Try repeating the original experiment, swinging the bull-roarer around slowly as you did before. But this time see what happens if you stand still while you swing the bull-roarer around, and the listener moves past the bull-roarer. (In this experiment, the listener should remove his or her blindfold.) Do you think the listener would hear a Doppler shift or not? The listener should still notice the Doppler effect, even though it is he or she, and not the sound source, that is moving.

Now, try this experiment again. This time both the sound generator and the listener should walk toward one another at roughly the same speed. If you do not have a partner, you can still do these experiments. Find a sound source that will make a steady note of constant pitch (such as an alarm clock). Set up the source outside on a chair so it is making a noise. Try walking or running past it at different speeds. Then try the same experiment with a sound source that changes in pitch, such as a radio playing music. Can you still hear a Doppler effect?

▶ *You can also hear the Doppler effect if you are moving, and the source of sound stays in one place.*

ANALYSIS
The Doppler effect

You should have found that when you were the listener, you could hear a distinct Doppler shift in the pitch of the bull-roarer as it moved past you. But when you were operating the bull-roarer, you should not have noticed any kind of Doppler shift; provided you swung the bull-roarer at the same speed throughout, the pitch of the sound should always have been the same. The Doppler shift should have been so noticeable that you were able to tell quite accurately the moment when the sound generator moved past you.

If you carried out the follow-up activities without any hitches, you should have found that the Doppler effect sounds the same whether it is the sound generator or the listener who is moving. When the person generating the sound and the listener walk toward one another, the Doppler shift should be even more noticeable. The Doppler effect depends on the difference in the motion of the sound generator and the listener. It is sometimes called the relative motion between them. If both are moving at the same speed, the effect is the same as if one person were moving faster.

Using a sound source with variable pitch, such as a radio, should not make any difference—you should still hear the effect.

Christian Johann Doppler

🔹 **Christian Johann Doppler noted how light and sound appear different when the object generating the light or sound is moving.**

The Doppler effect was named for Christian Johann Doppler (1803–1853), the Austrian physicist who discovered the effect. He noticed the effect of a moving object on the pitch of sound it produced and also predicted that this effect could be used to measure the speed of moving stars. That is because the Doppler effect does not just affect sound waves; other types of waves are also increased or decreased in frequency when they travel out from moving objects. Some stars in the sky appear redder or bluer than expected. Red light has a lower frequency than blue light. So if stars appear redder, they are moving away from Earth. Astronomers used this "red shift" to prove the universe is expanding.

🔹 **The light given off from moving gases in space shows the Doppler effect. Gas moving toward Earth gives off bluer (higher-frequency) light, while gas moving away from Earth appears redder (lower-frequency light).**

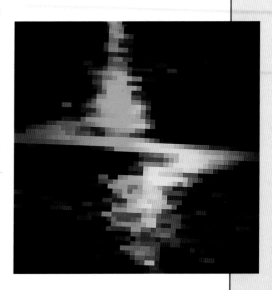

GLOSSARY

amplitude The height of a wave, such as a sound wave. The amplitude is half of the vertical distance between the peak and trough of the wave. The bigger the amplitude of a sound wave, the louder the sound.

antinode: A point in a vibrating object at which the vibration is greatest. It is also the point at which the sound wave has the largest amplitude.

astronomer: A scientist who studies outer space and the objects in space, such as planets and stars.

compression wave: A wave, such as a sound wave, that travels along a line rather than up and down. You can imagine it as the movement that travels along a slinky if you give one end a push.

constructive interference: When two sound waves meet in such a way that their peaks coincide and produce a sound wave of greater amplitude (louder sound).

decibel: A unit for describing the intensity of sound. Sounds of 130 decibels or more are painful for people to hear.

destructive interference: When two sound waves meet in such a way that the peaks of one do not collide with the peaks of the other—creating waves of variable amplitude.

echo: The repetition of a sound caused by the reflection of sound waves.

frequency: The number of times something happens in a certain time. The higher the frequency of a sound wave, the higher the pitch.

helium: A very light gas—it is lighter than the mixture of gases that makes up air and so is used to fill balloons.

humidity: The moisture content of the air.

insulate: To separate conducting bodies with nonconductors to prevent transfer of sound, heat, or electricity.

marimba: A xylophonelike instrument that originally came from southern Africa. Marimbas have resonators beneath each bar to make the sound richer.

molecule: A stable arrangement of two or more atoms.

node: A point in a vibrating object that is free of vibration. The amplitude of the sound wave at these points is zero.

percussion: Musical instruments that you strike.

phonograph: An early record player that reproduces sounds using the vibration of a stylus (needle) that follows a spiral groove on a revolving disk or cylinder.

piston: A sliding part. It is usually a short cylinder that fits snugly inside another cylinder that it moves back and forth inside.

pitch: Highness or lowness of sound. It is determined by the frequency of the sound wave.

pressure wave: A wave such as a sound wave created by a variation in pressure in the medium through which the sound wave then travels.

radar: A device that sends out radio waves. They are bounced back off distant objects, and in this way it is possible to create an image of the object. Radar is especially good for imaging the surface of planets and keeping track of the movement of aircraft.

radio wave: Part of the electromagnetic spectrum, like light and x-rays.

reflection: Sound or light "bounced" back off the surface of water, glass, metal, and so on.

refraction: Sound or light changing direction as it passes through water, glass, air, and the like.

resonance: Vibration of large amplitude that creates a rich sound. When an object resonates, it vibrates strongly with only a small stimulus.

resonant frequency: The frequency at which an object has to vibrate in order to resonate.

rotor: The rotating part of an electrical machine, for example, the blade of a helicopter.

shoal: A large group of fish.

shock wave: A compressed wave (such as a sound wave) caused by a disturbance like an explosion, an earthquake, or a supersonic plane.

sound barrier: A sudden increase in drag (the slowing effect of the air) as

an aircraft approaches the speed of sound.

sound wave: The way that sound travels through a medium. A sound wave is a compression wave.

standing wave: The pattern of vibrations in long, thin objects such as a string or a column of air (for example, in a flute or clarinet).

submarine: A naval vessel that operates under water.

supersonic: Any speed that is faster than the speed at which sound travels.

suspension bridge: A bridge that is partly supported by cables buried deep in the ground on either side of the gap.

taut: Having no give, being pulled tight. When some objects are taut, you can pluck them to make a sound—for example, the strings on a stringed instrument like a guitar.

transverse wave: A wave in which the vibration of the object is at right angles to the movement of the wave.

trawler: A type of fishing boat that has a large, cone-shaped fishing net trailing behind it. Trawlers are used for fishing along the seabed.

tuning fork: A metal instrument with two prongs. When it is struck, it makes a steady sound of one note. Tuning forks come in different notes, and they are useful for tuning musical instruments.

tuning peg: A peg on a stringed instrument around which a string is wound. When you turn the peg, the string becomes tighter or looser, affecting the pitch of the note that it makes when plucked or bowed.

vacuum: A space that is completely empty of matter.

vibration A regular movement of the minute particles in an object. A vibration, like a wave, is measured by its amplitude.

volume: The loudness (amplitude) of a sound.

vibraphone: A percussion instrument similar to a xylophone, but with metal bars and resonators driven by motors to produce an ongoing, rich sound.

wavelength: The horizontal distance between the peak of one wave and the peak of the next wave. In a sound wave, as the wavelength becomes larger, the frequency and pitch of the note also become lower.

SET INDEX

Page numbers in *italics* refer to pictures or their captions. **Bold** numbers refer to volume number.